THE HONEYBEE'S WAGGLE

Kelly Sargent

The Honeybee's Waggle

ISBN 978-1-970860-99-3

Cover Photo Credit: Kelly Sargent

ACKNOWLEDGEMENTS

Thanks are due to the editors and publishers of the following journals in which present or earlier versions of some included poems previously appeared:

Akitsu Quarterly, Autumn Moon Haiku Journal, cattails, Chrysanthemum, Circle of Salt, Cold Moon Journal, failed haiku, #FemkuMag, Fresh Out: An Arts and Poetry Collective, Frogpond, Haiku Dialogue, Haiku Girl Summer, Haiku in Action, haikuNetra Journal, hedgerow, The Heron's Nest, horror senryu journal, Kingfisher Journal, LEAF, Modern Haiku, One Art Haiku Anthology (2024 and 2025), The Pan Haiku Review, Presence, Rattle, tsuri-dôrô, and *Wales Haiku Journal.*

*For the survivor
in each one of us
who sips nectar once more*

THE HONEYBEE'S WAGGLE

PART ONE:
THE POLLEN

as though
this was forever...
the honeybee's waggle

thinking of you every daisy

first fireworks
the rosy hue
on lovers' glasses

counting down
to the wedding
white daisy days

how his mouth
holds my name
rose-brushed breeze

a rush of color
in my cheeks
winter kiss

wedding day sky
I borrow
something blue

chocolate fondue for two
double-dipping
the banana

when I was seen wild irises

analyzing his handwriting
his i
with a loophole

first anniversary refolding the paper airplane

French lavender bunch
the life I thought
I was bound for

between the birdsong
these secrets
I keep

PART TWO:
THE STINGER

my reflection in his eyes
when we quarrel—
how small i can be

fallen petals
how he used to
call me pretty

wiping the steam
from the mirror—
this longing to be enough

traveling the length
of my insecurity—
river murmurings

gathering seashells this wave of hollowness

the raven's caw
at twilight
before blue had a name

night swim spat...
the stars in my eyes
slipping through my fingers

sweet tea when he used to pick me wildflowers

h le in my p cket l st w nderment

straight seam stitches
the days I smile
only for selfies

walking on eggshells
the cracks
in this marriage

bringing our masks
to the table
mandarin mint mocktails

folding his socks mismatched
what I cannot
bring myself to say

vanishing point
the trap door
in his argument

tangled wind chimes
replaying
last night's words

winter sky swallows the words I cannot take back

even though
I said no
whentheriverrunsstill

civil twilight
the whispers
of witness trees

island sound waves of silence between us

frozen stream this desire to be stilled

wishing fountain
my prayers
caught in the downspout

pillowing our silence
for another night
winter fog

insomnia poems
adding to the narrative
of my shadow self

Escher's stairs
the steps I take
to go nowhere

utumn loneliness hearing the mourning dove out

finding
his hidden magazines—
paper cut

wading through
my insecurities
waist-high weeds

another's name
from his lips
spring snow squall

moonlit glen
the shadows
of his half-truths

the space between knowing
and not knowing...
winter rain

the punctuated pauses
in his confession
sunset thunderbolts

swallowing the words
I never expected to hear
starless night

her first name
the same as mine
blood moon

solar eclipse slivers
through the pine needles
the phase I cannot forgive

radiation frost—
the winter
we flatline

walking heel to toe
on a railroad tie—
the pros and cons list

snowflakes on my eyelashes
counting the reasons
to stick around

creeping ivy through the wagon handle
the decisions I make
by indecision

river bound raindrops
the alchemy
of suffering

wondering if this is
as good as it gets—
winter cherries

folding his socks
my way—
seasonal shift

black hellebores
adding drama
to the family soil

rabgrass on the garden's edge trial separation

the last leaf falling for lies no more

PART THREE:
THE HONEY

the day I leave blue morning glory

gypsy moth wanderings before my wings

wild fig tree bent seaward
longing once more
to long

root bound peace lily
the fear of letting go
of the fear

snow angel skirting around my demons

meteor shower
washing away
the night's friction

daring to believe
in something better
peach blossom buds

black magic hollyhocks
not believing
everything he tells me

letting go
of last night's words...
steeped black tea

tangerine sky
peeling the layers
of this thirst for more

nightingale's warble
my sobs
a little quieter

pawning the ring
the sapphire
a deeper shade of blue

rainfall at dusk...
the teardrop pearls
I leave behind

the lyrebird's cry
shedding yesterday
from my eye

melting snow
my winter shell
losing its hollow

sunbathing...
washing the clouds
from my thinking

leaving behind baggage cicada shells

newly divorced
the TV remote
in my hand

seaweed knots
on the surface
cleansing old wounds

pistachio shells
under the couch cushions
self-help workbook

spring rain the pitter patter of recovery steps

puddle reflections
the thoughts
I leave behind

practicing the pause
a patch of sunlight
on the cat's paw

peeling the sticker
from the garden hoe
the season I begin anew

polishing
the tarnished silver
divorcée's yard sale

making peace
an extra lemon slice
in the iced tea

strawberry shampoo suds
learning to care
for myself

first dress after the divorce
the twirl
of a single apple peel

morning mantra
softening the shell
of the seed

lotus in my palm
opening up
to my divinity

staying true
to myself
summer rain

questioning why no more shooting stars

sakura petals
in my glass
happy hour

braiding the silver
into the blue...
day stars

to live so fully summer sun shower

knowing safety at last morning murmuration

even after
all that's changed—
first bees

ABOUT THE AUTHOR

Kelly Sargent is a poet, artist, and editor living in the Green Mountain State of Vermont, USA. She is an assistant editor for *#FemkuMag*, and has served as a co-judge for the HSA Harold G. Henderson Haiku Award Contest (2025). Her poems have been honored in the Touchstone Awards long list, the Harold G. Henderson Haiku Contest, the H. Gene Murtha Senryu Contest, the Vancouver Cherry Blossom Festival Haiku Competitions, the Golden Haiku Poetry Contests, the Snapshot Press Calendar Contest, among others. She is the author of another haiku/senryu collection entitled *Bookmarks (Red Moon Press, 2023)*, and her works appear regularly in international short form poetry journals and anthologies.